Then & Now

Lower Town, Paducah

Judy Bray wrote the Lower Town Shuffle in 1983 to celebrate her neighborhood. She performed her song with other Lower Towners at the biannual Charity League Follies. Judy was an art and music teacher for 32 years. Every Sunday, she still plays the organ and directs the choir. She owns Fleur de Lis Antiques and Collectibles at 219 Kentucky Avenue. (Courtesy Judy Bray.)

THEN & NOW
LOWER TOWN, PADUCAH

Char Downs and Jay Downs Siska, Ed.D.

ARCADIA

Published by Arcadia Publishing
Charleston SC, Chicago IL, Portsmouth NH, San Francisco CA

Printed in Great Britain

Library of Congress Catalog Card Number: 2005908309

For all general information contact Arcadia Publishing at:
Telephone 843-853-2070
Fax 843-853-0044
E-mail sales@arcadiapublishing.com
For customer service and orders:
Toll-Free 1-888-313-2665

Visit us on the Internet at www.arcadiapublishing.com

Pictured here in August 1960 is Marjorie Green Blaisdell with, from left to right, her two sons, John M. and Owen K. (Kim), and her father, Owen R. Green, in the front yard of 521 North Seventh Street. (Photograph by Marjorie's husband, Jackson H. Blaisdell, Courtesy Kim Blaisdell.)

CONTENTS

ACKNOWLEDGMENTS

All photographs, unless noted, are by Char Downs. Prof. John E. L. Robertson started us on this adventure by recommending us to Arcadia. Ruth Walsh knows the names of all the houses and everyone in them. Penny Baucum Fields of the William Clark Market House Museum shared files and introduced us to many helpful Paducahans. Mary Hammond at the Paducah Convention and Visitors Bureau was a source of references and visitor statistics. Laura Lambert, St. Mary School System historian and teacher, tracked down facts of the academy. Elaine Spalding of the Paducah Area Chamber of Commerce opened that back room with boxes. Bill Crouch at the Alben Barkley Museum gave us free reign throughout the museum. Robert Shapiro—adventurer, photographer, downtown activist, and the only person we know to sail from Paducah, Kentucky, to Honolulu, Hawai'i—shared his unique "Faces of Lower Town" photographs, family information, and contacts. The Honorable Albert Jones, U.S. Army veteran, FBI agent, commonwealth and federal prosecutor, state legislator, mayor, and son of Paducah told us stories that made us laugh out loud. He knows everybody. Our adopted sister and brother, Charlotte and Ike Erwin, gave us the Lower Town Neighborhood Association files to review and showed constant interest. Teressa Hasty's work on the *Lower Town Walking Tour Guide* was a constant source of data. William Black Jr. showed his great humor and generosity in loaning us his family records of Lower Town. Mary and Bill Dyer let us in their cellar to go through boxes of photographs and memories. They also gave us access to their River Heritage Museum photographs. Dr. Scott Garrett told us stories of fascinating Kentuckians and was generous with introductions to those we would never have met otherwise. Gene Katterjohn told me stories with wit, insight, and patience. Zelma White, with her gentle hand, guided us through the files of her husband, Barron, on Paducah. Dorothy Barkley Holloway—granddaughter to the 35th vice president of the United States, Alben W. Barkley—opened her scrapbooks and boxes of slides, giving us a glimpse of a family that helped to change the world. The indomitable Mary Yeiser—artist, teacher, cofounder of the Paducah Art Guild (now Yeiser Art Center), and oldest living graduate of St. Mary's Academy at 100 years young on April 7, 2005—remembered stories of her art studies in Europe and life in Lower Town like it was yesterday. We are in awe of her. We got our photographs one or two at a time from each family. They invited us into their homes and told us of their proud heritage. They opened their shoeboxes, scrapbooks, suitcases, and cardboard boxes. We have truly been blessed to discover the place Char has been looking for all her life.

INTRODUCTION

This is a family album as much as a series of historical guideposts of Lower Town's place in history. When we could not verify historical data, we deferred to the family oral history. This is the first exclusive record of the emergence of this unique and vibrant community with restored homes, businesses, and retail art district. Use it as a companion to Images of America: *Paducah* and The Making of America: *Paducah*, both written by John E. L. Robertson and published by Arcadia Publishing.

Ardeth Fitzpatrick told us, "Lower Town is the overnight sensation that took thirty years to develop." It is a neighborhood being rebuilt by families who have been here for over 100 years, alongside those of us who have been here a little over 100 days. It is a community that welcomes artists from Maui to Massachusetts, from Puerto Rico to San Francisco, from across America and across town. There are also renovated live/work offices for lawyers, accountants, sheet metal businesses, insurance brokers, coffee houses, groceries, restaurants, and the new bus and trolley terminal. With all this change, some things remain the same. It still takes an hour to walk one block, stopping along the way to hear the latest news or check out what artists are working on in their studios.

The Artist Relocation Program started as an economic development initiative by the city to save the historic houses and buildings. It has grown into an economic attraction for artists and other professionals. There is no other artist relocation program like this in America. All of us are working together with the City of Paducah, Paducah Bank and Trust, and an army of overworked, happy building contractors. Thirty-nine galleries and studios are open and 15 more are under construction, with another larger group of artists and related businesses in the pre-construction phase. One hundred galleries are projected within a few years. Many of the remaining 233 buildings and lots in Lower Town are being renovated or built on by families returning to the neighborhood where their families first lived when they moved from Europe and across America.

In 1836, the Kentucky legislature passed an amendatory act to annex to the city of Paducah an area north of "Old Town," the commercial area. The addition was called "Lower Town" because it was downriver from Old Town. Paducah is in the western tip of Kentucky in McCracken County, where the Tennessee and Ohio Rivers meet.

The daylong Civil War battle of Paducah was fought in Lower Town. Over 60 houses were burned to the ground so that the attacking Confederates could not return and use the houses surrounding Fort Anderson to shoot over the fort's walls. Unable to take the fort, the Confederates burned the docks, took supplies, and left. It was a raid to force Union soldiers fighting in Atlanta to come to Paducah, giving the Confederate army a better chance of holding Atlanta. It did not work.

After the Civil War, Lower Town was the home for the downtown shop owners and merchants. Quality hotels and boarding houses were mixed in with grand Victorian and Queen Anne mansions. The hotels serviced the businessmen and entertainers from Wild West shows to operas traveling on the Ohio, Tennessee, Cumberland, and Mississippi Rivers. Broadway, the center of downtown, is just three blocks east of Lower Town.

Across the generations, various groups were responsible for reviving this neighborhood of tree-lined streets with houses and apartments in Italianate, Gothic Revival, Romanesque, and Classical Revival architecture. At times with visionary elected officials, at times with a focused city planning department, and at times with neighbors making their own way, Lower Town has survived with her own unique identity.

The latest reinvention may have begun with the beautification of downtown under Mayor "Dolly" McNutt (1972–1976). She and the business community, led by people like Robert Shapiro, worked to transform downtown into a tree-lined river city with new federal urban development funds and local contributions. Part of this program was to renovate above downtown shops and make quality rental units. Once downtown began to grow with small businesses, it set the stage for the formation in 1980 of the Lower Town Neighborhood Association.

Mayor Geraldine Montgomery (1988–1996) introduced the "Red Coat Ambassadors," a league of volunteers with Paducah in their blood and a gift for storytelling. "Gerry's Ambassadors" meet the riverboats and are present at functions to direct tourists. Later Mayor Albert Jones (1996–2001) promised to clear hazardous homes unfit for occupation. He came into conflict with preservationists, while others applauded his actions. In 2005, Mayor William Paxton is a champion of economic development. Thanks to consistent city leadership over the last 30 years, Lower Town has become a growing community of artists, businesses, and preservationists, participating in the national award-winning Artist Relocation Program—making Lower Town the fastest growing retail art community in America.

SELECTED MILESTONES FOR LOWER TOWN NEIGHBORHOOD ASSOCIATION

1980	Lower Town Neighborhood Association is formed.
1981	First Lower Town Fair.
	The Department of Interior lists the Lower Town Residential District on the National Register of Historic Places.
1982	First Candlelight Tour of Homes.
1983	Lower Town Garden Society names redbud the neighborhood tree and pink zinnia the flower.
1984	Paducah City Commission adopts a property tax moratorium to encourage restoration of historic properties.
1986	150th birthday of Lower Town.
	First time Lower Town is included on the official Dogwood Trail.
1987	The association produces *Trial by Jury* in the McCracken County Courthouse as part of the U.S. Constitution Bicentennial Celebration. It draws capacity crowds.
1988	First Lower Town Garden Walk.
1989	First regular horse-drawn carriage rides begin.

BIBLIOGRAPHY

Allen, Hall. *Center of Conflict, A Factual Story of the War Between the States in Western Kentucky and Tennessee.* Paducah: *Paducah Sun-Democrat*, 1961.

Brooks, Ora Bailey. *Brooks Bus Line: No Common Carrier.* Frankfort: Heritage Printing, 1985.

Growth Inc. *Lower Town: A Decade of Progress* newsletter. Paducah–McCraken County, Summer, 1990.

Holland, Richard. *Paducah: Portrait of a River Town.* Paducah: Image Graphics, 1992.

Langstaff, George Quigley Jr. *The Life and times of Quintus Quincy Quigley: His Personal Journal, 1859–1908.* Paducah: Paducah Area Community Foundation, 1999.

Lessley, Donald E. *Paducah Gateway: A History of Railroads in Western Kentucky.* Paducah: Image Graphics, 1994.

Neuman, Fred G. *The Story of Paducah.* Paducah: Image Graphics, 1979.

Paducah Department of Planning. *Lower Town Structure Inventory.* Paducah: City of Paducah, 1995.

Reed, Billee R. *A Score of Selected Servants: First Presbyterian Church 1842–1995.* Paducah: Farr-Better Supply, 1966.

Robertson, John E. L. *Paducah 1830–1980: A Sesquicentennial History.* Paducah: Image Graphics, 1980.

——. *Paducah: Frontier to the Atomic Age.* Charleston: Arcadia Publishing, 2002.

——. *Paducah.* Charleston: Arcadia Publishing, 2004.

——, ed. " 'High Water and Hell So Far:' A Paducahan Remembers the 1937 Ohio Valley Flood." *The Register of the Kentucky Historical Society.* 102.2 (Spring 2004).

Robertson, John E. L. and Margret B. *Fountain Avenue United Methodist Church, 1892–1992: A Centennial History.* Paducah: Image Graphics, 1992.

Wells, Camille. *Architecture of Paducah and McCracken County.* Paducah: Image Graphics, 1981.

White, Barron. *I Remember Paducah When . . . .* Paducah: Barrons Books & McClanahan Publishing House, 2000.

——. *My Paducah, from the Early Years to the Present.* Paducah: McClanahan Publishing House, 2002.

Chapter 1

EARLY
LOWER TOWN

For 50 years after the Civil War, Lower Town prospered as a residential neighborhood. Queen Anne, Greek Revival, and Italianate-Victorian homes were built. Shellie Leigh Bradford Geibel (sister of Wade A. Bradford and mother of Inez G. Burnett) and husband Henry lived in an Italianate-style home built in 1868 at 611 North Sixth Street. (Courtesy Buel Alexander.)

Quintus Quincy Quigley wrote in his journal, "James M. Mann and myself started the project of incorporating the town [of Paducah] into a city and extend the boundaries. At the first election under the charter in May 1857 I was elected city attorney." This 1903 portrait is with twin grandsons Samuel Husbands Langstaff (left) and George Quigley Langstaff (right) and Quigley's constant companion, his dog Bob Acres. (Courtesy George Quigley Langstaff Jr.)

Quintus Quincy Quigley (1828–1910) moved his family (daughter Ina seen at right in her 20s) to a log house built by Quigley at the corner of North Fourth and Monroe Streets. His father-in-law, James B. Husbands, gave them the property as a wedding gift. Later they moved to Fourth and Madison Streets. Today the homesite of one of the framers of the city's charter and the first city attorney is the Greyhound Bus Station. (At right courtesy George Quigley Langstaff Jr.)

After the Civil War, Confederate captain James T. Koger's family lived at 305 North Seventh Street and later at 725 Jefferson Street. He is shown above with five members of the Daughters of the Confederacy and his son, David. During the Civil War, Captain Koger rode in Gen. Nathan Bedford Forrest's cavalry. Koger was president of Paducah Wharf Boat Company. This example (at left) of Italianate architecture on Monroe and North Seventh Streets was built by Edward W. Vaughn around 1868. Vaughn also built the largest tobacco stemmery in western Kentucky two blocks away on North Fifth and Clay Streets. Today Vaughn's home is being restored as a single-family residence. (Above courtesy Louise Randle.)

American Revolutionary War major Charles Ewell was the 18th of 19 children of Betrand Ewell and Miss Kinnor. He is the grandfather of Charles and Thomas T. Ewell. Both fought for the Confederacy in the Battle of Paducah. The identity of the two adults and two children in front of Major Ewell's home on North Sixth Street in the *c.* 1900 image above is unknown. Today the home of these American warriors of the first battles on Lower Town's home soil is a property nestled among teenage trees. (Above courtesy Kentucky Historical Society.)

Fort Anderson was built by Federals around the Marine Hospital on the banks of the Ohio River at the foot of Lower Town, near North Fourth and Clay Streets. On March 25, 1861, Gen. Nathan Bedford Forrest led a Confederate army of 1,800 against 665 Federals, including freed African American slaves garrisoned at the fort. Hoping to weaken the Federals, Forrest placed Paducah-born soldiers at the front of the attack. The fort and hospital are long gone. A hotel and convention center occupies the space today. (Above courtesy Penny Baucum Fields.)

The Federals did not surrender. Confederates took cover and the higher ground. They shot over the walls from the second stories and roofs of nearby Lower Town homes. Failing to capture the fort, they withdrew. The next day, fort commander Col. Stephen B. Hicks ordered all homes within musket range of the fort burned to the ground. Sixty-six homes were destroyed. The Confederates never returned to Paducah to fight, but they did return to take horses. At right, a marker honors the 85 killed and wounded soldiers. (Above courtesy Penny Baucum Fields.)

This 19th-century home on Monroe and North Forth Streets stood on the site of the Roth Funeral Home, which was built in 1936. To the right of the two-story home is an example of one of the unique homes built in Lower Town. It is a one-story house with a two-story porch. In the summer time, before air conditioning, the second-story porch doubled as a bedroom for those hot August nights. The people in the picture are unknown. (Courtesy Tony Keeling, Roth Funeral Chapel.)

In 1997, Lindsey Funeral Home merged with Roth Funeral Chapel. The mini covered wagon traveling down Monroe Street has just come from the Labor Day Parade. Paducah loves parades. Parades are central to celebrating the holidays with balloons, happy children, marching bands, farm machinery, and all sizes of covered wagons, cowboys and girls, and Kentucky horses. All the parades move up the center of Downtown on Broadway and end in Lower Town.

In October 1858, St. Mary's Academy opened under direction of Sisters of Charity of Nazareth, Kentucky. In 1860, they purchased property on North Fifth and Monroe Streets from Judge George H. Morrow for the academy. It grew to the largest school in Paducah. The sisters closed the academy due to decreased enrollment 106 years later. In 1965, five schools and parishes combined into St. Mary School System. (Courtesy Laura Lambert, St. Mary School System.)

St. Mary's Academy was a pioneer in teaching art and music classes in elementary school. Above is a fifth-and-sixth-grade music class photograph from 1898. There were no public schools when the academy opened in 1858. Individuals conducted the few private schools in their homes. At right, the middle school band classes of today are gathered with instructors Douglas van Fleet and Patricia Story on the left. The academy and four schools that make up the St. Mary School System are now located outside of Lower Town on Elmdale Road in Paducah. The school is growing again. (Above courtesy Laura Lambert, St. Mary School System.)

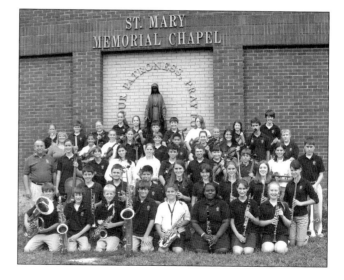

Jefferson Elementary School was built in 1890 at 418 North Eighth Street. Above is the second-grade class of 1927–1928. Caroline Finkel Jaffee (front row third from left), Herbert Wallerstein (back row fifth from left), and their teacher, Miss Williamson (right), are pictured above. Lower Town's children went here until 1965. Now they are bussed to newer schools in an expanded district. Today the site is part of the Paducah Area Transit System Terminal. (Above courtesy Caroline Finkel Jaffee.)

Built in 1897, the Colonial Apartments at 333 North Seventh Street derived its name from its distinctive façade featuring four huge Corinthian columns. Shortly after the end of the Civil War, Herman Wallerstein arrived in Paducah. He soon sent for his younger brother, Jacob Wallerstein, who at age 16 emigrated from their birthplace in Frankfort, Germany. In 1868, they founded Wallerstein Brothers, a men's clothier and downtown institution for 116 years. Brothers Herman and Jacob married sisters Fannie and Lulie Uri, and by 1897, they were living across the street from each other, Herman at 306 North Seventh and Jacob at the Colonial Apartments. Of the 333 buildings in Lower Town, a choice few have been maintained since they were built and look the same now as they did then. The Colonial is one of those buildings.

The year 1913 was one of great transition for the Wallersteins. In January, Jacob's first grandchild, Jeanne (Shapiro) (second from left), was born. In November, Herman's wife, Fannie, died. In December, Jacob's wife, Lulie, died. In 1915, Jacob's son, Melvin Wallerstein (far right), and his wife, Gertrude Wachtel Wallerstein (second from right), and infant daughter Jeanne moved into the Colonial with him. During the great snowstorm and influenza epidemic of 1918, Marie (Sommerfield) (middle) was born. Following Jacob's death in 1939, the family left Lower Town. Still attached to the Colonial, a slate memorializes original tenants, including Jacob (Jake) Wallerstein. (Courtesy Robert Shapiro.)

This 1850 Greek Revival house, one of the oldest in Lower Town, was built by Capt. William Smedley, a boat supply dealer and wharf master for the city. Later it was the home of David Ayers Yeiser. While mayor of Paducah from 1891 to 1897 and from 1901 to 1908, Yeiser obtained a charter as a second-class city, installed sewers and electric streetlights, and built the Market House and Riverside Hospital. He is the grandfather of Mary Yeiser. Today Yeiser's home on 533 Madison Street is owned by the Young Historians' Alben Barkley Museum, organized by Courtland "Eurie Pearl" Nell (woman with hat, on left). (Courtesy Bill Crouch, Barkley Museum.)

Chapter 2

MOTHER NATURE

Lower Town is no stranger to disasters. Nine major floods interspersed with ice storms have tested her residents. In February 1937, the Ohio River covered 95 percent of Paducah, cresting at 60.8 feet. Most residents were bussed to tent cities or neighboring towns. Here a Lower Towner strolls down North Seventh Street toward Madison Street—hip boots required. (Courtesy Bobby G. Smith.)

The spring flood of 1913 required 100 families to be evacuated. Water was about three feet deep in some parts of town. It was not as much a disaster as a nuisance to the folks who lived on the river. The city spent $6,000 out of local resources to cover damages. Paducahans used the flood as entertainment. It became known as a "Water Carnival," with decorated boats used in paddle races or leisurely Sunday spring afternoon boat excursions. These neighbors are out and dressed for the occasion and the camera on North Fourth Street in Lower Town. (Courtesy B. J. Summers.)

In 1937, the situation was much more serious. Coast Guard rescue boats picked up many stranded neighbors on their regular tours of Lower Town. Here nine Lower Towners and a guardsman seem to be looking down Monroe Street for survivors. Today the three-story apartment building on the left has been bought by Lou and Barb Barone and is slated for renovation into condominiums. The house on the right is now the law office of Charlotte B. Scott. (Above courtesy Mary and Bill Dyer.)

For many years, almost everyone in Lower Town was born in Riverside Hospital. This was the original site of the Marine Hospital that was encircled by Fort Anderson for protection during the Battle of Paducah. After the Civil War, the fort was leveled, but the hospital site remained. During the 1937 flood, this location so close to the river put the staff and its patients in harm's way. (Courtesy Penny Baucum Fields, William Clark Market House Museum.)

Under the direction of Rev. Dr. Frederick Olert, the First Presbyterian Church on Jefferson and North Seventh Streets was used as an emergency hospital for 180 patients from Riverside Hospital. Reverend Olert later helped to move these patients to higher ground at Clark School in the west end. All the churches assisted by housing patients from the flooded Riverside Hospital. (Courtesy Rev. Lynn Shurley, First Presbyterian Church.)

Capt. Louis Igert, his wife and business partner, Emma, daughter Julia, and their collie pose for a rare portrait. "Cup" Igert was a hero of the 1937 flood. Family history notes that he bought a railroad car of chickens and contents of two grocery stores for hospital use. His tugboat rescue fleet was used to collect stranded neighbors. Neighbors climbed from the second story of their home onto his barge to listen to flood news on a car radio. (Courtesy Mary and Bill Dyer.)

The corner of North Seventh and Madison Streets shows a side view of the Sinclair Gas Station and the Madison Apartments in the background with water at about the three-foot level. Today the gas station (later a Texaco) has been renovated by Mary Beth Young and Mark Barone to its Texaco design and is Julie Wagner's Candle Station. The Madison Apartments in the background are being renovated into condominiums. (Above courtesy Louis C. Kolb.)

On North Seventh Street, the row of businesses, homes, and a stranded car illustrate the remains of a previous snow. The Sanitary Cleaners was located at 414 North Seventh Street, and Benson's Grocery (with the two awnings and the john boat at the front door) was located at 416 North Seventh Street. Today there is a private park owned by Mary Beth Young and Mark Barone where the cleaners stood. Benson's Grocery eventually added a second floor. Today it is St. Luke's Press, a gallery and print studio. (Above courtesy Bobby G. Smith.)

The apartment houses on North Ninth Street between Monroe and Madison Streets were full of tenants. Within days, only 15 people were allowed to stay in all of Lower Town during the flood. They had permits for guns, boats, and entry. Today the two apartment houses remain, but the large double-porch home next door lost the battle of time and had no champion to rescue her. (At left courtesy Louis C. Kolb.)

The Coast Guard motor south on North Eighth Street just past Harrison Street with those they have rescued. The Tennessee Valley Authority came with approximately 50 rescue boats. Gov. A. B. "Happy" Chandler declared martial law in all of McCracken County and sent 23 officers and 344 men of the Kentucky National Guard. Looting was widespread. Boats were a constant target. Police and the National Guard convinced most of the residents to leave Lower Town and Paducah. (Courtesy Hal N. Sullivan.)

The Ohio River froze over in 1918. On January 10, 1937, an ice storm covered the county. Here bikers are lined up on the frozen water in January 1938, one year after the worst flood in Paducah's history. Below Bernie Hebert, Steve and Karen Utz, Michael Crouse, Teri Moore, Louis Lovera, and Cricket Alexander, the newest Lower Town neighbors, ride next to the Ohio River in the same location and take a rest at a riverside park. (Above courtesy Bill Crouch, Alben W. Barkley Museum.)

When the Ohio River froze in
1938, many residents drove
their cars and bikes to the river to
experience a walk on the frozen water.
Waterfront Lower Town is in the
background on the right. From left
to right, Dorothy, Stanley, and Marie
Stivers stand about 10 yards onto the
frozen river. The cars are parked on
the riverbanks. In January 2005, the
river rose again to just below the
floodwall. Photographer/author Char
Downs stands on the edge of the
rising waters. The water covered this
riverside park. (Above courtesy Dr.
Rupert Stivers.)

The Roth Funeral Home staff, Harry Earl Gilbert and Dee Denning (with oar), are pictured here leaving the 433 Monroe Street operation after spending another day cleaning and inventorying the flood damage. Years later, Harry Earl Gilbert would go on to realize his dream of working on the river by becoming a tankerman, just a year before he died. (Courtesy Harry Charles "Buddy" Gilbert.)

In 1934, William Osbourne bought Langstaff Lumber (previously Harwood-Derrington Lumber) at the corner of Clay and North Eighth. It became Osborne Hardware. During the 1937 flood, customers took supplies after Osbourne left for higher ground. When the flood subsided, the customers returned to settle their accounts. Two years after rebuilding, the store burned down. His family rebuilt again. In 1973, his daughter, Jane, and son-in-law, Nolan, bought it. Their son, Mike, suggested renaming it the Lumberteria. In 1998, Eldred Hurley bought the Lumberteria. It is one of the last family-owned hardware/lumber stores in Paducah. (Above courtesy Jane O. Harton.)

Plans began immediately after the 1937 flood to construct a floodwall. Construction began August 1939 under direction of the U.S. Army Corps of Engineers. Completed in July 1949, it consists of 13 pump stations, 9.3 miles of earth levees, and 3.1 miles of concrete wall. Fifty-five openings through the levee and concrete wall are sealed during flood periods with equipment maintained and stored at each opening. (Courtesy Kenny Brannon, Wayne Ryan, Mark Monroe, Greg Taylor, Robin Vaughn; Paducah Flood Wall Maintenance Department.)

Chapter 3
THE
NEIGHBORHOOD
FAMILY ALBUM

Historians, preservationists, teachers, shop owners, artists, lawyers, builders, doctors, investors, Civil War re-enactors, war veterans, chefs, and retired folks all found common ground. From 1980 to 1990, they held together to fight and sometimes agree with city policies in housing to preserve the historic buildings. The Lower Town Neighborhood Association held festivals, preserved homes, planted trees and flowers, did plays, threw parties, and fixed homes to be good neighbors. (Courtesy Lower Town Neighborhood Association.)

Hotel Craig, Paducah, Ky.

The Hotel Craig, later the Oxford Hotel, was a popular attraction and resting place for those traveling the Ohio River for business or pleasure. It stood at the corner of Monroe and North Sixth Streets. Paducah Bank and Trust leveled it in the early 1980s as part of a major reconstruction of the block. Today the main branch of Paducah Bank and Trust, the main lender and supporter of the Artist Relocation Program, occupies the location. (Above courtesy Roy Pelley.)

This *c.* 1875 Italianate home at 233 North Fifth Street was built by one of Paducah's leading attorneys, Sam Houston. Later Houston's niece, Pauline Houston Sevier, and her daughter, Dorothy Houston Sevier, lived there. Either Pauline or Dorothy stands by the fence. Today the house no longer stands, and this site is a beautiful park maintained by Paducah Bank and Trust. The bank preserved the single brick room that served as an outside kitchen for the house. According to local oral history, it was used as a jail during the Civil War. (Above courtesy Wally Bateman, Paducah Bank and Trust.)

In 1897, Alben William Barkley won the Oratory Award at graduation from Marvin College in Clinton, Kentucky. He would use his gift of speaking to motivate Congress and presidents to pass critical legislation in the years before and during World War II. He was a prosecuting attorney for four years, county judge for four, U.S. representative for 14, U.S. senator for 21 years—10 as the majority leader and two as minority leader—and vice president for Pres. Harry Truman. Below he gives his granddaughter, Dorothy, a kiss for winning "The Queen of Barkley Airport, 1949." (Courtesy Dorothy Barkley Holloway.)

In 1956, a crowd gathered at the Harris Funeral Home on the corner of Sixth and Monroe to pay their final respects to the late vice president. Barkley was brought back to his home and laid to rest in Mount Kenton Cemetery on Lone Oak Road, just a few miles from Lower Town. Today, in the lobby of Paducah City Hall, a bronze bust by Fredda Brilliant honoring Alben W. Barkley, vice president of the United States from 1949 to 1953, sits atop a marble monolith. The bust was funded by lovers of history and art and promoted by Lilija Macs Murphy in 1979. (Above courtesy Louise Randle.)

Sarah Smith Campbell lived on North Fourth Street (the man in the photograph is unidentified). She was known as the "Betsy Ross of Paducah." She designed and sewed the first Paducah city flag. Here she stands in front of 401 North Fourth Street, a previous homesite of the first city attorney, Quintus Quincy Quigley, and his family. In 2005, Sarah's homesite on Fourth Street is vacant and waiting for a new owner who might honor the previous residents. (Above courtesy Bill Crouch, Barkley Museum.)

The demolition of the Marks Apartments at Madison and North Seventh Streets was an example of over 411 buildings that were demolished by 1999 due to fire damage, poor maintenance, abandonment, or health hazards during the tenure of Mayor Albert Jones (1995–2001). Although controversial, it paved the way for new construction and opportunities in the beginning of the Artist Relocation Program. In 2005, this site is a well-maintained lawn waiting for a buyer to make the right deal with the owner for the next home or art gallery. (Above courtesy John E. L. Robertson.)

Ardeth and Pat Fitzpatrick bought this 1868 home on 321 North Fifth Street in 1957. They added a hair salon to the side and a garden with a koi pond. In 1991, Pat noticed a female cardinal hovering over the pond. He placed a stick across the pond. The bird used it as a perch to feed the fish. The bird—Ardeth called her Phoebe—returned every day for six seasons. The red bird only fed the red koi, never white koi. Local and national news programs picked up the story of Phoebe and her koi. (Courtesy Ardeth and Pat Fitzpatrick.)

Many Lower Towners move here because of the character of these old historic homes. They enjoy the challenge of a good restoration and the close-knit community of others who also respect and appreciate preservation. Will D. and Dorothy Mae Rogers (at right) were two such neighbors. They bought this one-of-a-kind 1877 home on 500 North Eighth Street in July 1989. They spent weekends and evenings tearing down, repairing walls and electrical, scraping paint, and restoring every part of their home. Six months after they finished their last project, Will died. Mae continues to work on their dream home. (Courtesy Mae Rogers.)

At left, Tom Rogers (left), the 19-year-old owner of Paducah Printing, is shown outside his 108 Broadway shop around 1910 with George Hazelbauer. Today located at 233 North Eighth Street, in a state-of-the-art complex of 38,000 square feet, Paducah Printing is a cornerstone of Lower Town business. Bruce Shulman and his mother, Alma Fritts, continue the tradition started over 100 years ago. (At left courtesy Bruce Shulman. Below courtesy Nathan Brown.)

In 1927, James Polk Brooks purchased a 1924 Plymouth. By 1929, he began driving passengers from Paducah to Detroit and back. It was 623 miles on rocky roads. By 1937, he owned a new DeSoto seven passenger that he would drive over a million miles. By the end of 1941, he had three 18-passenger busses. The Brooks Bus Service was the first tour bus to contract with the riverboats to take tourists around Lower Town and parts west. Today the trolley and busses of the Paducah Area Transit bring riverboat tourists through Lower Town. (Above courtesy Carol Brooks.)

A clay tennis court was excavated in 1917 to build the 306 North Eighth Street duplex named in honor of 1850s "Swedish Nightingale" opera singer Jenny Lind. P. T. Barnum brought her to America to select cities, including Paducah. In 1985, landscape architect Joanne Polk designed the formal gardens. In 1998, Cathy Crecelius and Steve Parrott converted it to a single-family home. Cathy was the first female president of the Rotary Club of Paducah in 2000. Steve directs newscasts for WPSD. Cathy is their director of promotions and public affairs. At left, Cathy (right) experiences a neighborhood perk, a marbling workshop with artist Charlotte Erwin.

Mary Yeiser worked as a store clerk downtown and dreamed of being a fashion illustrator. University of Kentucky art professor Edward Fisk told her, "If you are serious about art, go to Paris." Mary convinced senior Joy Pride to go with her. In Paris in 1928, they attended the Scandinavian Academy of Art, classes from Despujol and André Lhote, the Julian School, and the American Academy of Art. Bringing her love of art home, she graduated from Murray State Teachers College. Mary's lifelong mission was to teach and bring original art to Paducah. Mary, Virginia Black, and Bob Evans started the art guild later named the Yeiser Art Center (below) in her honor.

Inez Hardin proudly wears her Daughters of the American Revolution medals. She lived at this 1865 home on 509 North Sixth Street. She was the president of the Paducah Art Guild and was the music director and teacher at Paducah Junior College, where Mary Yeiser taught art. Today the home is a converted duplex rental with all the modern conveniences. It no longer has the beveled leaded glass windows, chandeliers, gaslights, or hand-carved oak doors. (Courtesy Robert Shapiro.)

Typical for Lower Town, the functions of structures change with the needs of the neighborhood. Louise and Howard Randle renovated the Fendley, Barker, and Harris Funeral Home on North Sixth Street in 1985. It is a prime example of well-maintained antebellum mansion. Mrs. Randle specializes in hand-made dresses and accessories of the Old South. (Above courtesy Louise Randle.)

Wanda and Thomas Sanders enjoy rehabilitating old homes and were drawn to Lower Town, where they had many choices. They bought the 1907 boarding house at 321 North Eighth Street and converted it into a single-family home. They kept the original exterior and remodeled the interior. Wanda (at left) works her magic with hammer, nails, lead, and stained glass in her "shed-io." "Other artists have studios," she says. Her home is a showcase for her art. Wanda's stained glass creations are also installed in homes throughout Lower Town, Paducah, and Nashville, Tennessee.

This Queen Anne Victorian at 304 North Seventh Street with a Russian dome has been carefully maintained to showcase its original design. The extensive perennial gardens are the pride of the neighborhood. Herman Wallerstein built the house in 1895. The current owner, leathersmith Philip Philips, has preserved the design and construction of both the interior and exterior of his Dixie Rose. It is on the federal register of historical homes and is the showroom and leather craft shop for Dixie Leather Works. He produces museum-quality reproductions of handcrafted leather items historically documented from the 1832–1876 period. For 15 years, he has made props for the entertainment industry.

The 1897 building on 630 North Sixth Street was the Three Arch Grocery and later an ice cream shop. The first-floor façade was typical of commercial structures from 1860 to 1890. This façade has a cast-iron J. H. Johnson Foundry threshold. Second-floor round-arched Italianate windows are rare. In 1984, Brenda Stansberry and Sharon Clymer opened American Harvest Antique Shop, rescuing another vacant historic Lower Town building. (Courtesy Sharon Clymer.)

A great Lower Town landmark is this Queen Anne Victorian home on North Ninth Street with a pyramidal roof and an octagonal corner tower built by George C. Wallace in 1889. He was a local vinegar works owner then vice president of the Paducah Railway and Light Company. It was later used as a boarding house. Norma and Curtis Grace made it one of the Top 25 Restaurants in *Southern Cuisine*, and Curtis was one of America's Top Chefs (1992–1994). Today Jay Solomon is restoring the mansion as a gallery and residence for artists visiting and researching moving to Lower Town. (Above courtesy Jay Solomon.)

Remodeled in 2001, Paducah Area Transit System (PATS) Terminal (below) at 850 Harrison is an example of transit officials and government working together bringing jobs and redevelopment to a neighborhood. The leadership of Senators Mitch McConnell and Jim Bunning and Rep. Ed Whitfield, working with the local transit system, earmarked funds to improve transit service buy buses and vans and construct a terminal. An Access to Jobs grant from the Federal Transit Administration allowed busses to run after hours, helping night workers access child-care and jobs. Additional funding from the grant provided streetlights, sidewalks, and a park-and-ride lot. (Courtesy Gary Kitchin, PATS.)

Chapter 4

THE ARTIST
RELOCATION
PROGRAM

In 1999, Mayor Albert Jones sent City Commissioner Robert "Buz" Smith, Planning Director Tom Barnett, and Lower Town artist Mark Barone to Rising Sun, Indiana, to see how artists helped in restoring a community. They returned with enough interest to begin the Artist Relocation Program in August 2000. Most artists started with abandoned buildings (above). (Courtesy Connie Noyes.)

This 1860 home of riverboat captain Andrew Fritts and his wife, Mary, had an upstairs porch for a river view. It was one of the few two-story houses left after the fires were set from the Battle of Paducah. Time and river air had not been kind to this old house. (Courtesy Terrie Runyons.)

Terrie Runyons moved to Paducah after falling in love with the town during several visits to her friends and former neighbors, Patience and Bill Renzulli. She bought her pre-Civil War home on Madison Street sight unseen from photographs Patience e-mailed to her. Terrie's love of gardening and talent at decorating has brought the house back to its former glory. The front rooms of the home now serve as a charming gift store, A Dog In the Garden, which Terrie and Patience own and operate together.

John Sinnot, a road construction contractor, and wife Elizabeth built this Romanesque Revival home on 228 North Ninth Street in 1888. In the 1970s, it was converted to apartments, then a law firm. Today it is the home of Beverly Hayden and Angled Art Gallery. Beverly took singing lessons here when she was in high school. Later, while preparing for law school, she delivered documents from her law firm to the attorney practicing out of this house. When Beverly (at left) heard of the Artist Relocation Program through artists already participating, she knew what building she wanted for her own gallery.

The 1873 home at 502 North Sixth Street had been converted during the Depression to apartments. Now it is the Global Nomad Coffee House and Global Gifts and home for Monica and Paul Bilak and their children, James, Jonathan, and Chloe. For three years, Monica taught special education, and Paul was a nurse practitioner at Rift Valley Academy in Kenya, Africa. In 2002, the Bilaks returned to America. They were in Nashville for three months both looking for jobs and a place to put down roots. A friend told them about the program. In 2004, after extensive renovations, they opened Global Nomad.

This house on 527 North Sixth Street is a famous residence in Lower Town. During the 1937 flood, a *National Geographic* photographer saw a cow on this second-story balcony. The photograph was published worldwide. Jim Huston lived here and was taking care of the cow for a friend. He pointed the cow towards the stairs and crimped her tail; the pain of bending her tail made her run up the stairs to safety. Grace and Bernie Hebert are rehabilitating this house into the Stranded Cow Restaurant and Gifts. Grace is working on a new piece of jewelry by flattening a strand of silver over a round metal support.

San Juan, Puerto Rico, is the birthplace of Aynex Mercado (at right). She met her husband, Rob Cook, at the University of Massachusetts in Amherst. Aynex was the first quilter based in Paducah to be accepted into the American Quilters Society Annual Quilt Show in its 21st year. Rob and Aynex read about the Artist Relocation Program on the Internet at an art magazine Web site. They bought the building at 335 North Sixth Street (above) that Mary Yeiser lived in for many years. It will become their home and Galeria Aynex to showcase a variety of her quilts. (Above courtesy Ruth Walsh.)

George and Sarah Barnes bought the land for 524–536 Harrison Street around 1860 and built the duplex before June 1864. In 1884, Quintus Quincy Quigley arranged for the sale of the property from George Barnes to Mary Watson, Francis Jones, and Thomas Jones. The deed lists Barnes's purchase price of "$135 in hand." Barnes organized the 16th Kentucky Cavalry. During the Battle of Paducah, Maj. George Barnes had the job of burning down houses in Lower Town near Fort Anderson after Forrest's raid. This may be why this two-story duplex survived the fires. (Courtesy Mark Palmer.)

Today one of the very few remaining pre–Civil War residences on Harrison and North Sixth Streets and the earliest known multi-family dwelling in Lower Town is the home, artist retreat, and fine art gallery of Mark Palmer. Mark learned about the program in late 2001 from Craig Kittner and planned a visit for early 2002. Excited about the renaissance in Lower Town, Mark relocated in September 2002. The gallery offers a unique steel floor designed and installed by Washington, D.C., artist Chet Holcomb. The Mark Palmer Gallery showcases two and three dimensional art and installations from both national and international artists. New exhibits rotate every two months.

This classic 1882 Greek Revival home was built for Frank M. Fisher by his father, three-time mayor of Paducah John C. Fisher (elected 1863, 1865, and 1875). Frank M. Fisher was a campaign manager for William McKinley's first successful presidential campaign. After McKinley's election, Fisher was appointed McCracken County Postmaster on February 16, 1898. (Courtesy Julie Shaw.)

Julie Shaw has created fine jewelry for 25 years. Her brother Tim, a musician in San Francisco, told her about artist friend Paul Lorenz moving to Lower Town. He urged her to see the program's Web site. She read, visited, and bought. Julie moved from the Four Corners region of southwestern Colorado to 503 North Seventh Street in 2004. She converted the front rooms (above) into Aphrodite Gallery to showcase her jewelry work with stones and metal along with other American fine craft artists. Rosie, her Chinese crested dog, surveys the gallery. Julie uses a soldering torch (at left) for another work of wearable art.

This 1885 apartment house at 403 North Seventh Street stands at the center of Lower Town. It started as a single-family residence. Over the years, it was halved and halved again to accommodate the influx of uranium plant workers and river dock construction workers in the 1940s and 1950s. Here 1937 flood victims await a boat to take them and their dogs to higher ground. (Courtesy Bobby G. Smith.)

Born in Morocco the youngest of six children in a military family, Lorrie Cody grew up living in different places. Deciding engineering would be a practical vocation, she had a very fulfilling career at Hughes Aircraft in El Segundo, California. The left side of the brain finally gave in to the creative side when she saw an article in an art magazine about the program. It made her laugh; she kept it in her planner. It led to a visit to Paducah in May 2002; she moved here October 2002. Today LOCO Art Gallery showcases her work and other artists.

In 1936, the Benson Food Store at 416 North Seventh Street provided free delivery to Lower Town neighbors. Here "Big Jack" Benson is taking his son, "Little Jack," and a neighbor's daughter for a test ride. The Benson Food Store served Lower Town for 30 years. (Courtesy Jack Benson.)

Today the Benson Food Store has become the home of Mark Barone, printmaker and Artist Relocation Program coordinator, and Mary Beth Young, author and college librarian. Recently they completed their first collaboration, a book of etchings and contemplative verse titled *Christ's Passion: The Way of the Cross.* Here Mark, in his studio with Santina, checks a print he has hand pulled from his Rembrandt press.

An unfortunate circumstance of vacant buildings is that glass doorknobs, brass plating, historic ceramic tiles, and cast-iron fireplaces grow legs in the night. Copper pipes and claw-foot tubs sprout wings. Other houses suffer spontaneous combustion. These phenomena plagued Lower Town buildings. The houses at 418 and 420 North Seventh Street were no exceptions. They were stripped of all reusable materials. There was nothing left for Berkeley, California, architect Louis Lovera and artist Paul Lorenzto to do but tear them down and design a new building complex that fit in with the neighborhood and would accommodate their professions. (Above courtesy Louis Lovera.)

Louis (right) has begun to experiment with clay. In such a diverse and artistic community, it is common for artists to gather ideas and techniques from others to incorporate into their own art forms. Paul's work (below) is on display at STUDIO mars, 418 North Seventh Street. He continues to teach graduate school classes in abstraction for the Academy of Art University, located in San Francisco and online. Galleries in San Francisco, New York, and Europe represent Paul's work.

Originally from Kentucky, Freda Fairchild moved from San Diego after hearing about the Artist Relocation Program while she was working with artist Judy Chicago on an art installation at Western Kentucky University in Bowling Green. She drove to Lower Town, fell in love with this house at 328 North Eighth Street, and bought it the first day. She became the one of the first out-of-town artists to arrive here as part of the program. Freda is an internationally known artist and founding member of the Paducah Printmakers. The front rooms of her home showcase her prints, quilts, and paintings.

This Queen Anne home was built in 1900 at North Seventh and Trimble Streets (now Park Avenue) by J. A. Bauer, owner of Paducah Pottery Works. He employed 35 workers processing 50,000 gallons of clay each month. He started the world-renown Bauer Pottery Company in Los Angeles. Now the Queen Anne is the home of Nathan and Nicole Brown, their children, and Nathan's Centered Studios. His ceramic art is showcased here. Nicole owns Paducah Yoga Center on North Seventh and Broadway. Nathan is an outdoorsman, musician, graphic artist, Paducah Tilghman soccer coach (regional champions 2005), vice president Paducah Film Society, and director of the annual River's Edge Film Festival of Independent Films.

In 1897, Anton List was a prominent druggist in Paducah. He is shown here with one of his three daughters at 322 North Eighth Street. The interior of his pharmacy was known for intricate wood banisters, railings, and cabinets, which were donated by Ethel Dubois Smith to the Market House Museum in 1963, when the pharmacy closed. (Courtesy Madora Irion Hoff, from collections of William Clark Market House Museum.)

Christian artist and Paducah resident Teresa Perry heard of the program from Nathan Brown. She bought the List home. Teresa apprenticed with master woodworker and carver Charles Richard "Dick" Baucum. It was Baucum, with the support of his daughter, Penny, and wife, Alice, who voluntarily restored and reassembled the elaborate interior woodwork of the List Drug Store at William Clark Market House Museum after the museum's 1974 fire. A finish carpenter by trade, Teresa is a woodcarver, sculptor, painter, antique restorer, and reproduction specialist. To display her artwork, the front rooms of her house are now Agape Studio. When she purchased the house, she was unaware of its history.

The corner of Monroe and North Eighth Streets is an example of architectural recycling. The lot was first purchased by the Hopkins family of Christian County, Kentucky. Mr. Hopkins built the first house in 1867. In 1898, his daughter, Georgia, and her husband, Robert L. Eley, built their home, a Queen Anne–style Victorian cottage, using some of the original materials from her childhood home. The Eleys owned a dry goods store on Broadway. They sold the house to E. S. Barger, first president of the Board of Directors of Western Baptist Hospital. (Courtesy Ike and Charlotte Erwin.)

One hundred years later, Kentuckians Charlotte and Ike Erwin took one look at this house and looked no further. They became the first artists in the program. They spent the next four years carefully restoring the house. It became a gallery and studio for their work and a home with son Erick Allen. Charlotte is a musician, marbler, painter, and nationally certified museum art framer. Musician and bookbinder Ike produces "hero props" for the movie and television industry. At right, Charlotte applies pigment on top of "heavy water" for marbling a silk scarf. Below Ike performs a little country, blues, and rock and roll.

Craig Kittner surfed the Web for a new home. He found www.paducharts.com. Craig and wife Denise Gordon visited Lower Town from Washington, D.C. They saw this building with room-size holes in the floors and ceilings, crumbling walls, and four feet of water in the basement; Denise said, "I don't care, this is it." They immediately saw past the ruin of this dilapidated 1850s building at 329 North Fifth Street and were determined to turn it into a fine dining restaurant, Café Minou; a studio for Craig, Kitt Art Studio; and their home. (Courtesy Craig Kittner and Denise Gordon.)

Denise Gordon comes from a second-generation restaurant family and is a sous chef. She graduated from the University of North Carolina, Charlotte and the College of Culinary Arts at Johnson and Wales University. Her husband, Craig Kittner, is a graduate of the University of Tennessee with a degree in marketing. Craig has an extensive exhibition record in the mid-Atlantic area.

This 1897 home at 803 Madison Street housed a beauty parlor and apartments in 1999, when it was gutted by fire. In 2002, Dr. William "Bill" Ferrar Renzulli spotted an ad in an art magazine that would bring him, his wife, Patience, and nine Warburton whippet dogs from Elkton, Maryland, to this abandoned shell. Patience and Bill created a home, writing and sewing space for Patience, and an art studio and Gallery 5 for Bill. Gallery 5 features Bill's work; his oldest daughter Amy's jewelry; and the paintings of his youngest daughter, Sara. Bill's middle daughter, Beth, continues the family legacy as a physician. (Courtesy William Ferrar Renzulli.)

Bill and Patience were the third family to move into Lower Town in the Artist Relocation Program. Patience is author of *Mama Pajama Tells a Story*, a collection of short stories of her life with whippets and Bill. She loads up the dogs in their travel trailer and makes the rounds of field trials and dog shows throughout the year while researching her next book. At right, Patience (center) is showing champion Warburton Falcon Calls (also known as Logan). Below, Bill Renzulli's range of work includes watercolor paintings of historical buildings, three-dimensional collage structures, and abstract clay monotypes. (At right courtesy Patience Renzulli.)

One of the most dramatic construction projects to improve a property exterior was accomplished by Keyth Kahrs and Elaine Spalding in 2002. They took this 1877 two story with a second-story sleeping porch and converted it into a single porch with two-story columns. Now it is Leaping Trout Studio and their home on Harrison Street. (Courtesy Keyth Kahrs.)

K eyth met Elaine in Oregon. She was moving back to her home state of Kentucky to be president of the Paducah Chamber of Commerce and he was on his way to Tucson to be a graphic artist for the Yellow Pages. Elaine kept telling him about the new Artist Relocation Program. Their two-year long-distance courtship ended when Keyth moved to Paducah to marry Elaine. Keyth has put down the mouse and computer for the brush and canvas.

Connie Noyes read an ad in a now-defunct Chicago art magazine about the program. She was ready for a change. With her son, Alex Mariano, and her psychologist husband, Bob O'Brien, they moved from San Francisco in 2003. They restored this four-unit 1857 building at 614 Madison Street into a single-family home, art studio, gallery, and apartment for visiting artists. (Courtesy Connie Noyes.)

Connie earned a master of fine arts degree from the School of the Art Institute of Chicago and a master in art psychotherapy from Notre Dame de Namur University. Currently she is working with an encaustic process of pigment and wax. Connie is part of a 17-member international contemporary abstract painters group, Pintura Fresca. Connie states, "As an intuitive painter, my paintings lie in the core reality of struggle and chaos. From this core I work to extract a sense of elegance and hope. Trust in the process and a profound connection to the act of painting itself are what activate this shift in my work."

Ray Black built this house at 521 Madison Street for John Owen in 1925. This was the first contract for a company that is still building in Paducah today. Ray's son, Bill, joined the company in 1947, and the name was adjusted to Ray Black and Son. Some houses in Lower Town were put together from other structures, and since this is a river town, some were built from boats. This home has a number of cross beams with a definite nautical purpose. Today Ray's grandsons Bill Jr. and Chris, grandson-in-law Rick Coltharp, and great-grandson David carry on the family business. (Courtesy William Black Jr.)

Nancy Calcutt found out about the program in 2000 from an art magazine advertisement. She was an art professor at a college in Southern Mississippi. She showed her husband, Charlie Doherty, the ad, and they were on their way. They built an addition following the same architectural design as the original house. It contains Dancing Dog Art Studio and Gallery and Red Stag Recording Studio. Charlie has been an active performing singer/songwriter 30 years. Nancy works in a contemporary realistic style depicting scenes of animals, people, and nature. She is also Charlie's muse and a singer in his band.

This is a result of the 1994 demolition of St. Mary's Academy Chapel on Monroe Street. Eleven years later, this end of Lower Town has come alive again thanks to Michael and Kama Rannells from Chicago. They read about the program in the *Chicago Tribune*. In 2005, they opened Loaf, Inc., a specialty grocery store and deli at 420 Monroe Street. Michael, a drummer and video technician, and Kama, an interior and fashion designer, run the store. The renovation has transformed the music wing of the academy into the first specialty grocery store and deli in the Artist Relocation Program. (Above courtesy Lower Town Neighborhood Association, below courtesy Michael Rannells.)

INDEX